MARTIN LUTHER KING JR.

MARTIN LUTHER KING JR.

A Man with a Dream
by Jayne Pettit

A Book Report Biography
FRANKLIN WATTS
A Division of Grolier Publishing
New York / London / Hong Kong / Sydney
Danbury, Connecticut

Cover illustration by James Mellett

Photographs ©: AP/Wide World Photos: 47 (Charles Gorry), 15 (Gene Herrick), 67; Archive Photos: 23 (George Tames/ New York Times Co.), 51; Corbis Sygma/Gregory Pace: 11 right; Corbis-Bettmann/UPI: 2, 8, 11 left, 19, 32, 33, 63, 74, 89, 94; Folio, Inc./Jeff Greenberg: 30; Liaison Agency, Inc./Hulton Getty: 79; Magnum Photos: 83 (Bob Adelman), 68 (Danny Lyon); Morehouse College: 39, 97.

Visit Franklin Watts on the Internet at:
http://publishing.grolier.com

Library of Congress Cataloging-in-Publication Data

Pettit, Jayne.
    Martin Luther King, Jr. : a man with a dream / by Jayne Pettit.
        p.   cm.—(A book report biography)
    Includes bibliographical references and index.
    ISBN: 0-531-11670-0 (lib. bdg.)   0-531-15553-6 (pbk.)
    King, Martin Luther, Jr., 1929–1968—Juvenile literature. 2. Afro-Americans—Biography—Juvenile literature. 3. Civil rights workers—United States—Biography—Juvenile literature. 4. Baptists—United States—Clergy—Biography—Juvenile literature. [1. King, Martin Luther, Jr., 1929–1968. 2. Civil rights workers. 3. Clergy. 4. Afro-Americans—Biography. 5. Civil rights movements—History.] I. Title. II. Series.

E185.97.K5 P44 2001
323'.092—dc21
[B]   00-036646

GROLIER
PUBLISHING
1 2 3 4 5 6 7 8 9 10 R 10 09 08 07 06 05 04 03 02 01

CONTENTS

CHAPTER ONE

"THERE COMES A TIME WHEN PEOPLE GET TIRED"

On Monday, December 5, 1955, an event took place in the city of Montgomery, Alabama, that would forever change the course of United States history. It happened quietly and without fanfare, cheerleaders, marching bands, or lengthy speeches by the city's political leaders. No guns were fired and no lives were lost. And the most amazing thing about this momentous event was that

On that cold winter day long ago . . . the civil rights movement in America's Deep South began in earnest.

no one would have predicted that it *could* have happened.

On that cold winter day long ago, the Montgomery, Alabama, Bus Boycott—when thousands of the city's Negro citizens refused to ride on segregated buses—was the start of the civil rights movement in America's Deep South. It was a courageous course of action because tragic things had happened to African-Americans in the South who had taken a stand against cruelties and injustices that denied them their constitutional rights.

Little more than a year had passed since the United States Supreme Court had outlawed segregation in public schools, and tensions between

This photograph shows an interior view of an empty Montgomery city bus stopped in the center of town during a busy workday. It is a sign of the success of the Montgomery Bus Boycott.

whites and blacks were high. In cities and towns throughout the South, White Citizens Councils were forming to block desegregation and people were taking the law into their own hands. Hate groups such as the Ku Klux Klan (KKK) night riders terrorized black neighborhoods, firing shots into people's homes and burning crosses on their lawns.

In Montgomery just three years before, Jeremiah Reeves, a young drummer in a black high school band, was accused of sexually assaulting a white woman. An all-white jury found Reeves guilty and sentenced him to hang. Despite appeals by the local chapter of the National Association for the Advancement of Colored People (NAACP), the boy was later executed. People throughout Montgomery's Negro community were enraged by the tragedy, because it was a well-known fact that white men in the city—including several white policemen—had sexually assaulted Negro women and had been found not guilty of all charges.

By late January 1956, the Montgomery Bus Boycott had been underway for more than a month. In the kitchen of his little white parsonage, twenty-six-year-old Martin Luther King Jr., the recently appointed pastor of the Dexter Avenue Baptist Church, sat with his head in his hands, and a steaming hot cup of coffee rested untouched on the table in front of him.

Hours before, he had crawled into bed, exhausted from weeks of anxiety and the burdens of leadership he had reluctantly accepted. Arriving home after a stormy meeting of the Montgomery Improvement Association, he had answered yet another crank telephone call, forcing himself to listen as a muffled voice on the other end of the line drawled, "Nigger, if you aren't out of this town in three days, we gonna blow your brains out and blow up your house."

A cold chill had swept through Martin as the receiver clicked. Pacing the floor as the caller's words raced through his head, the young minister had finally reached a decision: He would resign from the presidency of the association the next morning. He would put a stop to the obscene phone threats and the hate letters that were pouring in. Many of them were signed by the KKK.

Struggling to clear his mind of the heavy responsibilities he had undertaken, Martin thought of the thousands of African-Americans who were risking their lives every day by refusing to ride on segregated city buses. Some of these people were walking from homes as far as twelve miles away to get to their jobs as maids or gardeners or other types of laborers. Still more were riding to work in mule-drawn wagons or sharing their cars and trucks with neighbors. Because of him, fifty thousand people, dependent upon the

Coretta Scott King in 1968 (left) and in 1996 (right)

buses as their only affordable means of transportation, were participating in a crisis that seemed to be going nowhere. Where would it all end?

Unable to sleep, Martin had gotten up and walked to the kitchen to brew a pot of coffee. Sitting down at the table as the first light of day broke through the window, he had bowed his head in despair. He thought of Coretta, his young wife, and Yolanda, their two-month-old baby girl, and feared for their safety.

Then, from somewhere inside him, something seemed to tell Martin that he must not let his people down. They needed him and depended on him to lead them through these difficult times. Martin began to pray aloud:

Oh, Lord, I'm down here trying to do what is right. But, Lord, I must confess that I'm weak now. I'm afraid. The people are looking to me for leadership and if I stand before them without strength and courage, they too will falter. I am at the end of my powers. I have nothing left. I can't face it alone.

Minutes later, Martin became aware of an inner voice that seemed to be telling him to stand up for truth and justice for his people. The voice was calm and reassuring, and as he listened, his fears gradually disappeared; he felt stronger than he had in weeks.

Several nights later, Martin was speaking before a large group at one of the mass meetings of the Montgomery Improvement Association. In the middle of his address, someone rushed up to tell him that his home had been bombed. As his audience sat in stunned silence, Martin quietly excused himself and left the meeting.

Arriving at the house, the young minister saw hundreds of angry people milling about in the street. Pushing through the crowd, Martin found Coretta and the baby shaken but unharmed. Then, stepping up to a section of the porch that was still standing, he spoke to the people, many of whom were carrying guns and bottles and shouting at the swarms of police that had arrived on the scene.

> My wife and baby are all right. . . . I want you to go home and put down your weapons. We cannot solve this problem through retaliatory violence. . . . We must meet hate with love.

Someone later described the reaction of the crowd that night. Amazed at the remarkable calm and quiet force with which Martin had addressed the people, the person said, "He held up his hand, and they were suddenly silent . . . absolutely still."

The Montgomery boycott was not the first of its kind to protest the harassment of innocent blacks riding on city bus lines. Two years earlier, a group in Baton Rouge, Louisiana, had used nonviolent action to protest segregated public transportation. In 1942, James Farmer's Congress of Racial Equality (CORE) had used nonviolent direct action to oppose racial discrimination in public services, public accommodations, and housing in Chicago, Illinois.

What had sparked the Montgomery movement was the arrest of Mrs. Rosa Parks, a forty-two-year-old tailor's assistant working in one of the downtown department stores. Mrs. Parks, an intelligent and highly respected woman, had been the secretary of the Montgomery chapter of the NAACP and was well known in the Negro community.

At the end of a long day at work, Mrs. Parks had stopped briefly at a nearby drugstore and then boarded a crowded rush-hour bus to find a seat just behind the Whites Only section. After making one or two stops, a number of white people got on, and seeing that there were no seats left, the driver ordered Mrs. Parks and several other Negroes to turn their places over to the white riders. After a moment or two, the other Negroes stood up, but Mrs. Parks remained where she was. When the driver ordered her to do the same, she refused. A short time later, Rosa Parks was arrested.

"I had had problems with bus drivers over the years, because I didn't see fit to pay my money into the front and then go around to the back. Sometimes bus drivers [all were white] wouldn't permit me to get on the bus, and I had been evicted," Mrs. Parks told a news reporter years later.

What had happened to Rosa Parks that evening was a familiar story to countless blacks in the cities at that time. For years, they had been the victims of harassment and insults. Women

Rosa Parks is fingerprinted by a Montgomery deputy sheriff following her arrest for refusing to give up her bus seat to a white passenger.

took the greatest amount of abuse, frequently being ordered to pay at the front, leave the bus, and then board at the back door. In one incident, a driver allowed an elderly woman to enter and then slammed the door on her blind husband, dragging him for several feet before stopping the bus.

Because Rosa Parks was so well known in the Negro community, word of her arrest on that December evening spread rapidly. Among the first to hear the news was Jo Ann Robinson, president of the Black Women's Political Council. After a brief discussion with her associates, Mrs. Robinson phoned E.D. Nixon, head of the Montgomery chapter of the NAACP, and urged a boycott of the city's buses in protest of Mrs. Parks's arrest. Nixon agreed and quickly arranged for Mrs. Parks's immediate release on bond, with a trial set for the following Monday.

The next morning E.D. Nixon telephoned Martin to tell him that Rosa Parks had been charged with violating the Alabama segregation law. Nixon was excited because he knew that as a result of the Supreme Court's ruling of the year before, he had a solid federal case in his hands. "We can go to the Supreme Court with this and boycott the bus line at the same time," he said. "Make it clear to the white folks we [aren't] taking this type of treatment any longer."

That evening, leaders from the Negro community met at Martin's Dexter Avenue Church to schedule the boycott for the following Monday. That allowed enough time for word to spread and for Mrs. Robinson and her organization to distribute thousands of copies of a leaflet she had written calling for a one-day bus boycott. The city's eight Negro taxi companies would also be asked to transport workers for the same cost as the ten-cent bus fare. A second meeting would be set for Monday evening, when a decision would be reached as to how long the boycott should last.

By dawn on Monday, Martin waited anxiously for the first bus on the South Jackson line to pass in front of his house. Concerned about the risks his people were about to take, he had little sleep the night before. As he drank his morning coffee, he kept thinking about what might happen. What if the people panicked and backed out? What if the boycott failed?

At 6:00 A.M. a bus that was normally loaded with domestics came into view. From the living room, Coretta suddenly called to him, "Martin, Martin, come quickly!"

Running to the front window, Martin watched excitedly with his wife as the first bus of the day passed by the house. It was empty. Fifteen minutes later, another bus with no riders on board moved past. Soon after a third vehicle came along, empty except for one or two white customers. Martin could not believe what was happening. Jumping into his car, he drove to the home of his friend, the

Reverend Ralph Abernathy, the minister of another of the Negro churches. Together the two drove up and down the city's streets. Everywhere they looked, the buses were empty. The boycott was working!

Other things were happening as well. Black cab drivers, some seventy altogether, were carrying people to work for the same ten-cent fare that the buses charged. College students attending Alabama State were cheerfully hitchhiking along the way and schoolchildren were standing at bus stops shouting, "No buses today!" as empty buses passed. Three hours later Martin and Ralph Abernathy arrived at City Hall to attend Rosa Parks's trial. A police squadron carrying sawed-off shotguns stood facing a huge crowd of blacks waiting silently to hear about the trial.

After a short session that morning, the court found Mrs. Parks guilty and fined her $14. But E.D. Nixon was jubilant, filing immediately for an appeal to the federal district court—the first step in a legal battle that would ultimately reach the Supreme Court.

That afternoon, Martin and other leaders gathered together to form the Montgomery Improvement Association (MIA), an organization that would oversee the boycott for as long as it would last and also act as a watchdog for any racial problems the community might face in the future. Martin reluctantly accepted the presiden-

Reverend E.J. Fields, secretary of the Montgomery Improvement Association, was an integral part of the organization's management of the boycott.

cy saying, "Somebody has to do it. And if you think I can, I will serve."

When the young minister arrived at the Holt Street Baptist Church to address the first meeting of the Montgomery Improvement Association, he was astounded to find thousands of people waiting to hear what he had to say. Loudspeakers were ready to carry his words to the crowds standing outside in the cold. Martin worried that he had not had enough time to prepare his speech, but within minutes he was speaking to his people without a single note in front of him:

> We're here this evening for serious business. We're here in a general sense because first and foremost, we are American citizens, and we are determined to acquire our citizenship to the fullness of its meaning. We are here also because of our deep-seated belief that democracy transformed from thin paper to thick action is the greatest form of government on the earth. . . . We are determined to get the [bus] situation corrected. . . . But there comes a time when people get tired. We are here this evening to say to those who have mistreated us so long that we are tired—tired of being segregated and humiliated; tired of being kicked about by the brutal feet of oppression. . . . If we are

wrong, the Supreme Court of the United States is wrong. If we are wrong, God Almighty is wrong. . . . If we are wrong, justice is a lie.

To the thousands of people listening to Martin Luther King's words that night, a new day was dawning. The young man standing in the pulpit before them was telling them that their future could be brighter. He was giving them hope and pleading with them to stand together for the cause of justice and freedom.

As the enthusiastic crowd cheered and interrupted him with shouts of praise and "Amens," Martin Luther King sounded his first call to nonviolent direct action, insisting that theirs would not be a movement that condoned violence. Theirs would not be an imitation of the White Citizens Councils or the KKK. He reminded them that the road they were about to take would demand courage, endurance, and the risk of injury and perhaps even death.

In our protest there will be no cross burnings. No white person will be taken from his home by a hooded Negro mob and brutally murdered. There will be no threats. . . . We will be guided by the highest principles of law and order. . . . If we protest courageously, and yet with dignity and Christian love, when the history books are written in the future, somebody will have to say, "There lived a race of people, of black people, of people who had the moral courage to stand up for their rights."

Rufus Lewis, one of the African-American community's most able leaders, later said of Martin's address, "This was the time that the people were brought face to face with the type of man that Martin Luther King was. . . . That was the great awakening. It was astonishing, the man spoke with so much force."

The meeting that night at the Holt Street Baptist Church marked the beginnings of what Martin himself called "the Miracle of Montgomery," when "thousands of black people stood revealed with a new sense of dignity and destiny."

A three-point resolution was adopted that evening. The Montgomery Improvement Association demanded an end to the harassment of blacks by bus drivers, a first-come, first-served policy for all passengers, and finally, the immediate employment of black bus drivers on predominantly black workers' routes. Until those demands were met, the people would refuse to ride on the city's buses.

On the following Thursday, Martin and other

Martin Luther King Jr. addresses the congregation at Holt Street Baptist Church in Montgomery.

members of the MIA met with city officials to present the resolution, pointing out that a policy such as theirs was already working in three other segregated cities in the South. When the resolution was turned down, the MIA vowed to continue the boycott.

In the weeks that followed, the blacks of Montgomery suffered countless hardships as they trudged back and forth on foot or rode their mule-drawn wagons. When the city refused to allow black taxi drivers to charge their ten-cent fare, the drivers, Martin, and the MIA formed car pools at forty-eight dispatch and forty-two pickup stations to transport workers who needed transportation.

Many blacks took pride in "demonstrating with their feet." One old woman, refusing the offer of a ride, answered proudly, "I'm not walking for myself, I'm walking for my children and my grandchildren!" When Martin urged an elderly member of his congregation to stop walking and accept a ride, she told him she was going to walk until the boycott ended.

"But aren't your feet tired, Mother Pollard?" Martin asked.

"Yes, my feet is tired, but my soul is rested," she replied with dignity and a new sense of hope that the future would be better for her people.

There were times during the boycott when that kind of hope seemed to fade, despite the courage of the African-American community. City officials began harassing the MIA's leaders, and the KKK stepped up its violent activities throughout Negro neighborhoods. The home and church of Martin's good friend, Ralph Abernathy, had been bombed along with three other churches. Martin had been arrested for driving five miles over the city's speed limit. Hate mail and death threats had started pouring into his home. When told by a friend that rumors were circulating about a plan to have him assassinated, he admitted that he was deeply afraid. Then came that remarkable night when Martin had felt that strong, inner voice urging him to press on for his people.

As the months dragged on, city officials tried to break the boycott by accusing Martin and hundreds of black leaders of violating a law forbidding such action. At a grand jury trial in March 1956, Martin was found guilty and fined $500 for inciting his people to break the law. But the boycott, now receiving national attention in the papers and on television, continued.

Throughout the spring, a battle raged between an Alabama circuit court that ruled segregation on the buses was legal according to state law and a federal court that asserted bus segregation violated citizens' rights as guaranteed by the Constitution's Fourteenth Amendment. While the courts argued the case back and forth, Martin traveled from coast to coast answering invitations to share the "Montgomery story" with audiences eager to hear about his people's fight for their constitutional rights.

By early November, the city of Montgomery blocked the MIA from operating the car pools carrying blacks to work, claiming that they were both a "public nuisance" and a "private enterprise" operating illegally without a license. Martin was desperate and felt that he had let the protesters down.

"I'm afraid our people will [have to] go back to the buses," he told his wife. "It's just too much to ask them to continue if we don't have transportation for them."

On November 13, Martin was in court again. A judge fined the MIA $15,000 for organizing the boycott. It seemed that the end had come. "The clock said it was noon," he later remembered, "but it was midnight in my soul."

Then a startling thing happened. While Martin was conferring with the MIA's NAACP lawyers, he heard a rustling in the courtroom and a reporter from the Associated Press raced up the aisle to greet him. "Here is the decision you've been waiting for," the reporter exclaimed breathlessly. "Read this release!"

Martin could hardly contain himself as he read the statement:

The United States Supreme Court today affirmed a decision of a three-judge U.S. District [federal] Court in declaring Alabama's state and local laws requiring segregation on buses unconstitutional.

The people of the African-American community in Montgomery were thrilled when they heard the news. "God Almighty has spoken from Washington, D.C.," someone was heard to say. But later that day, when it was learned that white extremists in the city were organizing for violence, everyone agreed to a secret plan of action.

When forty carloads of white-robed and hooded Klansmen roared through black neighborhoods that night, the people—who for years had always locked themselves in their homes and turned off lights at the first sign of trouble—now stood in their Sunday-best clothes on brightly lit porches, waving and cheering at the cars as they went by.

"They acted as though they were watching a circus parade," Martin remembered later. "No one fears the Klan or the White Citizens Councils."

On December 20, 1956, one year and three weeks after the arrest of Rosa Parks, a copy of the Supreme Court order arrived at the capitol building in Montgomery. That same evening Martin addressed a mass meeting of the MIA, urging his people to continue to avoid violence in the weeks ahead:

As we go back to the buses, let us be loving enough to turn an enemy into a friend. We must now move from protest to reconciliation. It is my firm conviction that God is working in Montgomery. Let all men of good will . . . continue to work with him.

CHAPTER TWO

"YOU ARE SOMEBODY!"

Martin Luther King Jr. came into the world on January 15, 1929. The second child and the first son of the Reverend and Mrs. Martin Luther King Sr. of Atlanta, Georgia, "M.L." had made such a quiet entrance that his doctor thought something might be wrong.

But the doctor's fears were short-lived, and within a few years, M.L. was busy doing what all little boys loved to do: ride bikes, build model airplanes, and fly kites outside his home on Auburn Avenue, a quiet, tree-lined street in the heart of the prosperous, middle-class African-American community. The people called the area "Sweet Auburn" because its residents were the pride of black Atlanta—teachers and college professors, doctors, lawyers, and ministers who were the community's highly respected leaders.

A park ranger talks with visitors in front of the Atlanta, Georgia, house where Martin Luther King Jr. was born. The house has been restored and preserved as an historic attraction today.

M.L.'s father, the Reverend Martin Luther King Sr., was the pastor of Ebenezer Baptist Church, a congregation he had inherited from his late father-in-law. The son of a poor sharecropping farmer and a cleaning woman from central Georgia, Daddy King had left home at a young age and walked all the way to Atlanta with nothing but the clothes on his back.

Arriving in Atlanta, Daddy King worked at a number of odd jobs before deciding that he wanted to be a preacher. Soon he was traveling between two small churches, serving each as pastor while attending night school to get his high school diploma. Hardworking and fiercely independent, he eventually earned his bachelor's degree from Morehouse College, one of several fine African-American colleges in Atlanta.

One of the people in the black community Daddy King most admired was the Reverend Adam Daniel Williams, the father of Alberta Williams, a young woman he had been dating. Born to slavery, Williams had been freed by Lincoln's Emancipation Proclamation and had risen to become pastor of Ebenezer Baptist Church. A strong and inspiring preacher, he was a charter member of the Atlanta chapter of the NAACP, an organization that used the power of the courts to fight the evils of segregation.

Martin Luther King Sr., better known as Daddy King

Alberta Williams King, Martin Jr.'s beloved mother

On Thanksgiving Day in 1926, Daddy King and Alberta Williams were married, and shortly after, Daddy King was appointed assistant pastor of Ebenezer Baptist Church. Three wonderful children came along, first Christine, then M.L., and finally, "A.D.," named in part after his grandfather Williams.

When M.L. was two years old, The Reverend Adam Daniel Williams died suddenly, and Daddy King took his place as senior minister at Ebenezer. A gifted speaker with a mind for business, Daddy King attracted thousands of new members to the congregation, expanded the church's facilities, and raised the number of choirs to six, with Alberta directing from her seat at the organ. A man of boundless energy and determination to succeed, Daddy King also found time to become an active member of the NAACP, earn his doctor of divinity degree, and serve as a director of a prominent African-American bank.

"They went out of their way to provide everything for their children."

The home that Martin Jr. knew as a child was a happy one. His parents loved and respected one another and each had a distinct role in the household. Daddy King, a strong, patriarchal father, rewarded his children for good deeds and jobs well done. His wife, Alberta, a quiet, affectionate woman known as Mother Dear, left disciplining the children to her husband. In addition to the three children, there was also Grandmother Williams, Alberta's mother, who spun magical moments on Sunday evenings with her spirited stories from the Bible.

Years later, Martin Luther King Jr. recalled that innocent, untroubled time in his life:

> The first twenty-five years of my life were very comfortable years, very happy years. . . . I didn't have to worry about anything. I [had] a marvelous mother and father. They went out of their way to provide everything for their children.

The Kings also did everything they could to protect their children from the indignities of the South's rigid segregation laws. Daddy King, who refused to ride on segregated buses, also avoided public restrooms and drinking fountains marked Colored Only or Whites Only. As a result, M.L. and his sister and brother knew nothing about these insults in their earliest years.

But one day, when the parents of M.L.'s best friend told him that he could no longer play with their son, the little six-year-old asked why. "Because we are white and you are colored," they answered to his dismay.

Later M.L.'s parents described the two worlds that the people of the South lived in: One was white and the other colored, with separate schools, movie houses, stores, churches, neighborhoods, and public facilities. "As my parents discussed some of the tragedies that resulted . . . and some of the insults they themselves had confronted . . . I was greatly shocked, and from that moment on I was determined to hate every white person," Martin Luther King Jr. later wrote.

But M.L.'s mother quickly urged him to remember who he was. "You must never feel that you are less than anybody else," she told him. "You must always feel that you are somebody!"

In time, M.L. entered school and did well. A bright child with an inquisitive nature and an easygoing manner, he moved through the grades quickly, skipping a couple and entering high school younger than most students his age.

But M.L. quickly discovered the pain of segregation was always present. With the generous allowance money he received each week from his father, M.L. bought Cokes, french fries, and cheeseburgers from a colored store, watched the latest movies from filthy upstairs balconies marked For Coloreds Only, and stood at a side window of the nearest drugstore to accept his ice cream "cone" in a paper cup. Despite his thirst for books like everyone else in his family, he was denied entrance to the public library.

When M.L. saw KKK night riders for the first time and learned of the lynchings of blacks in Atlanta, he was enraged. When his parents tried to tell him to love all people because it was his duty as a Christian, he would challenge them by saying, "How can I love a race of people who hate me?"

M.L. vented his anger on the neighborhood ball fields with his teenage friends, one of whom later commented that in football, "[Martin] wound up as a fullback" despite his small size "because he ran over anybody who got in his way." Another buddy reported that "he could outwrestle anybody in our gang . . . and he knew it."

Along with his great love for books and sports, M.L. loved to dance, played the violin, and developed a passion for opera and jitterbugging. He excelled at subjects such as history and English. But the ugly specter of racism continued to haunt him. Entering a speaking contest in his junior year, M.L. traveled ninety miles away with his English teacher to address a group on the subject of African-Americans and the Constitution. He won the contest easily and later the two boarded a bus for the long ride home. On the way, the bus became crowded when a number of white passengers entered. M.L. and his teacher were told to give up their seats. When M.L. refused, the driver called him an insulting name. At his teacher's insistence, the young man rose to his feet, and he and his teacher stood for the rest of the trip. "That night will never leave my mind," King said years later. "It was the angriest I have ever been in my life."

The desire to help his people was strong because of what he and other blacks were experiencing in the South in the early 1940s. "I was at that point where I was deeply interested in political matters and social ills," he remembered. "I could see the part I could play in breaking down the legal barriers."

One year later, M.L. entered Morehouse College after skipping his senior year of high school. He became a college freshman at the age of fifteen. Throughout his years at Morehouse, M.L. kept the plight of African-Americans at the forefront of his mind. Of the many fine professors with whom he studied, the person who had the strongest influence on him was Dr. Benjamin Mays, the college president. A champion of racial justice, Mays helped the young man to realize that education was the most important tool for social change. A theologian and a writer, Mays influenced M.L. with his intellectual approach to the ministry.

When he first had begun his studies, M.L. had resisted the idea of becoming a minister like his

A view of Graves Hall, the first building on the campus of Morehouse College

father and his grandfather. He felt that the fields of medicine or law would give him a better opportunity to bring justice to his people. But Dr. Mays showed him that he could be most effective as a minister. "I came to see that God had placed a responsibility on my shoulders," the gifted young student later said.

From Morehouse College, Martin went on to Crozer Theological Seminary, just outside Philadelphia, studying with enthusiasm and devouring philosophy as well as the works of the great theologians of the past. One evening he heard a lecture by Mordecai Johnson, the president of Howard University, a prestigious school for blacks in Washington, D.C. Johnson had just returned from a trip to India to study the teachings of Mahatma Gandhi, the great leader whose "Soul Force" movement of nonviolent resistance had brought down the power of English colonialism in India. It was a night that changed the course of Martin Luther King Jr.'s life.

Completing his studies at Crozer Seminary, Martin headed for Boston, determined to earn a doctorate in systematic theology before beginning his ministerial duties. While in Boston, he met a beautiful young woman who was doing graduate work at the New England Conservatory of Music. On their first date he took her to the cafeteria on the school campus, and while they were eating lunch, he announced that he was going to marry her. Martin said she had everything that he wanted in a wife—beauty, personality, character, and intelligence.

"I don't see how you can say that," the young woman answered. "You don't even know me."

The young woman's name was Coretta Scott. On June 18, 1953, Martin and Coretta were married by Daddy King at Coretta's family home in Marion, Alabama.

CHAPTER THREE

"GIVE US THE BALLOT"

After their marriage in Alabama in the summer of 1953, Martin and Coretta returned to Boston to finish their graduate degrees. Throughout the fall and spring terms, they discussed where they might live. Both loved Boston because of its fine colleges, its libraries and museums, and the opportunity to attend the symphony and the theater. During frequent walks through the city's lovely parks, they talked about their future together.

He was increasingly concerned about the black community's acceptance of the humiliations of segregation.

Martin told Coretta of his dreams of teaching in a university surrounded by his books, his students, and his world of ideas. Perhaps he would take a church position for the first few years; he loved ministering to people and helping them with their struggles, just as Daddy King had done in Atlanta for years. Coretta knew by this time that she would not fulfill her own dream of becoming a concert singer. But she had adjusted to that and told Martin that she would support him in whatever he decided to do.

When the Dexter Avenue Church in Montgomery called Martin that spring to serve as pastor, the young couple faced their first serious dilemma. For years they had studied and lived in the North, enjoying the freedom of the university campuses each had been a part of. As an undergraduate student at Antioch College in Ohio, Coretta had been a member of that college's chapter of the NAACP and was active in its race relations and civil liberties committees. She had also felt the sting of prejudice when a local public school board denied her a position as a student teacher because she was black. By moving back to the South, both she and Martin knew they would once again experience the pain of second-class citizenship.

After weeks of discussion, Martin and Coretta made the decision to accept the church's offer. They would serve in Montgomery for a few years and then return to the academic world in the North.

When Martin took over his church responsibilities in Montgomery in September 1954, the Supreme Court's ruling on school desegregation was the subject of heated debate throughout the Deep South. Determined to keep things as they had been since 1896 when the same court had ordered "separate but equal" education for Negro and white students, White Citizens Councils backed by the Ku Klux Klan were doing everything possible to prevent schools from desegregating by the beginning of the fall term.

As they settled into the little parsonage a short distance from the church, Martin and Coretta forced themselves to adjust to the hostile environment of the Deep South once again. Coretta put her musical talents to good use by joining the church choir and gave numerous concerts in cities throughout the area. She also began taking an active role in Martin's pastoral and community commitments by becoming his secretary. Meanwhile, Martin's reputation as a gifted speaker was spreading throughout the Negro community and beyond.

By September 1955, Martin was active in racial affairs in Montgomery, serving on the executive board of the local chapter of the NAACP and the Alabama Council on Human Relations, the city's only interracial organization. But as time passed, he was increasingly concerned about the black community's acceptance of the humiliations of segregation. Little did he know that this attitude was about to change because of one woman's quiet determination to assert her rights and defend her dignity as a human being.

On November 17, 1955, the Kings' first child Yolanda, was born. In December the nationwide news coverage of the Montgomery Bus Boycott gave thousands of southern blacks the courage to begin working for change. Within days of the Supreme Court's mandate, similar protests led by other black ministers took place in Birmingham and Mobile, Alabama, as well as in Tallahassee, Florida.

Then one day in January 1956, Bayard Rustin, an African-American pacifist and civil rights activist in New York who had acted as an advisor to the MIA during the Montgomery boycott, telephoned Martin to suggest that they form a new organization that would unite cities throughout the South in the struggle for racial equality. This group would work with other groups such as the National Urban League, the NAACP, and CORE.

During the next several months, Martin and Bayard Rustin contacted ministers in each of the Southern states to establish a group that would teach Negroes their constitutional rights and encourage voter registration so people would have a voice in local and state government.

On May 17, 1957, Martin joined with Roy Wilkins of the NAACP, A. Philip Randolph, the leader of the Brotherhood of Sleeping Car Porters, and other black leaders from around the country to celebrate the third anniversary of the Supreme Court's decision to integrate public schools. This

Pictured (left to right) at the May 17, 1957 Freedom Pilgrimage rally at the Lincoln Memorial in Washington, D.C.: Roy Wilkins, Martin Luther King Jr., and A. Philip Randolph.

was called the Freedom Pilgrimage rally. Speaking from the steps of the Lincoln Memorial in Washington, D.C., he told an audience of close to 40,000 people that the time had come to give African-Americans a voice in the affairs of the government:

> Give us the ballot . . . and we will fill our legislative halls with men of good will . . . give us the ballot and we will place judges on the benches of the South who will "do justly and love mercy," and we will place at the heads of the Southern states governors who will [work for black equality] . . . the hour is late. The clock of destiny is ticking out. We must act now, before it is too late.

In August 1957, 115 black leaders met in Montgomery to form the Southern Christian Leadership Conference (SCLC) that Martin and Bayard Rustin had been working on. This organization would be different from other black organizations in that it would be made up entirely of local affiliates, each of which would send delegates to its national conventions. Martin was elected president by unanimous vote.

By this time, the young minister was working twenty hours a day, and gaining national attention as he traveled from coast to coast to address the plight of African-Americans throughout the country. Martin had also appeared on the cover of *Time* magazine along with a feature article describing him as "scholarly, personally humble, articulate and of high educational achievement."

With speaking engagements, interviews, and press conferences taking up more and more of his time, Martin struggled to attend to his church duties and to be with his family. In his small office at the parsonage, the phone rang constantly, giving him little privacy to work on his first book, *Stride Toward Freedom*, the story of the Montgomery Bus Boycott. The dream of a university professorship seemed very far away.

When an invitation arrived from Kwame Nkrumah, the American-educated prime minister of the new republic of Ghana, Martin recognized an opportunity to get away for a couple of weeks and visit one of the earliest African nations to emerge from the shackles of European colonialism. During their stay, Martin, Coretta, and the stately Nkrumah talked about American and African blacks and their common struggle for equality.

In September, a racial battle took place in Little Rock, Arkansas. A federal court ordered the integration of nine black students at Central High School. However, Orval Faubus, the state's governor, ordered the Arkansas National Guard to prevent the students from entering the building. Later, newspapers from around the country printed front-page photographs of fifteen-year-old Elizabeth Eckford trying to move quietly past a hate-filled mob of men and women screaming insults and spitting on her freshly laundered dress. As the situation worsened, President Dwight D. Eisenhower, who had not yet taken a stand in support of school integration, was forced to send armed paratroopers to the city to protect Elizabeth and the other students.

Martin called the incident "a tragic revelation of what prejudice can do to blind the visions of men [and women] and darken their understanding."

In October a far happier event occurred when the Kings celebrated the birth of their second child, a boy. Martin and Coretta named him Martin Luther King III.

By February 1958, Martin and other civil rights leaders launched their Crusade for Citizenship, aimed at doubling the black vote in the 1960 presidential election. As he worked to raise funds for the campaign, Martin declared, "We feel that one of the most decisive steps that the Negro can take at this time is that short walk to the voting booth."

Addressing a huge crowd in Miami, Florida, on Lincoln's birthday, Martin said, "Let us make our intentions crystal clear. We must and we will be free. We want freedom now. We want the right to vote now."

Several months later, Martin made the

nation's news headlines when he was arrested once again, this time on a false charge of loitering and refusing to obey a police officer. Physically assaulted by angry white police, he was later released but brought to trial, where he was ordered to pay a fine of $10 or serve a jail term of two weeks. When Martin chose the jail term, the police commissioner, in an effort to avoid further publicity, paid the $10 fine himself.

In the fall of 1958, Martin was in New York for interviews on several television and radio programs to promote the publication of *Stride Toward Freedom*. Later, while signing copies of his book at one of the city's department stores, a mentally ill black woman stabbed him in the chest, causing a near-fatal wound. Rushed into surgery, Martin survived, only to learn that the tip of the blade had rested on the main artery to his heart.

While Martin was recovering, thousands of letters of support poured in from all over the world, many of which were sent by white people. Coretta later remembered that her husband's favorite was from a young white high-school student who wrote, "I read that if you had sneezed, you would have died. . . . I'm so happy that you didn't sneeze."

Coretta's role as Martin's secretary and chief supporter during this time was rapidly increasing. In addition to keeping up with the massive

During the Kings' visit to India, Martin met with that country's prime minister, Morarji Desai.

amounts of mail that arrived each day, she had begun traveling around the country giving freedom concerts for the benefit of the civil rights movement. Her efforts were a huge success, raising thousands of dollars for the cause. In 1958 she addressed the Youth March for Integrated Schools in Washington, D.C.

In February 1959, the Kings flew to India to meet with followers of Mahatma Gandhi and to study Gandhi's philosophy of peaceful opposition.

Speaking to huge crowds who turned out to hear him, Martin told of the African-Americans' struggle for freedom and equality, pointing to the example Gandhi had set for them in their own nonviolent protests.

Returning to Montgomery, Martin announced to his congregation that he was resigning from the Dexter Avenue Church in order to take up a copastorship with his father in Atlanta. Telling his people that freedom was "always purchased with the high price of sacrifice," he pleaded with them to continue their work for justice "until every black boy and girl can walk the streets with dignity."

CHAPTER FOUR

ON FIRE FOR FREEDOM

On February 1, 1960, four Negro college students in Greensboro, North Carolina, shocked waiters at a Woolworth's department store when they asked for service at the store's lunch counter. When told to leave, the students politely refused and stayed in their seats while a policeman paced back and forth behind them, pounding his billy club into the palm of his hand.

The sit-ins were not the first to take place in the country, but they were the most effective.

The students involved in this peaceful confrontation had planned their action with care. Their challenge was a simple one: Why should state laws deny them the freedom to eat with whites in public places when the same laws gave them the freedom to buy merchandise from which those same places made a profit?

The next day, more than twenty other students joined in the lunch counter protest, occupying most of the seats and asking to be served. It was a peaceful demonstration by students who said they were influenced by Gandhi's philosophy of nonviolent protest.

Within a short time, students from several of the area's colleges—many of them white—joined what became known as the sit-ins at Greensboro's lunch counters and restaurants. When owners tried to solve the situation by removing chairs and stools, the young people stood, taking shifts that lasted until closing time. Thousands later demonstrated at shopping centers and drive-in movies in the area, quietly, politely, and peacefully asking to be served. Before the end of that year, public eating facilities in Greensboro were finally desegregated.

The sit-ins were not the first to take place in the country, but they were the most effective, giving black students in the South the courage to join in the protest.

In Nashville, Tennessee, James Lawson, a young black minister doing graduate work at Vanderbilt University, was teaching classes on Gandhi's philosophy of nonviolent protest. Lawson had studied Gandhi's work while serving as a missionary in India, and his goal was to encourage students to confront racial barriers with peaceful resistance. Inspiring his students with Gandhi's

Hindu principles, Lawson's aim was to get students involved in the civil rights movement in an organized way.

In his workshops, Lawson also taught the young people how to defend themselves if they were physically beaten. Among the tactics Lawson taught were how to curl themselves up to protect vital organs, to look directly into their assailants' eyes—a tactic Gandhi had proven to be confusing, even embarrassing, to an attacker—and to protect one another in such a situation.

Many of Lawson's students wrote to Martin asking for advice on the eve of their first protest. Martin, in turn, told the students that their sit-in movement was "one of the most significant developments in the civil rights struggle."

When Martin learned that a college sit-in back in Montgomery had been broken up by police who later attacked the students' college campus with tear gas and sawed-off shotguns, he telegraphed President Eisenhower to "take immediate action . . . to restore law and order." The president, however, ignored Martin's request.

Later, in articles for *U.S. News & World Report* as well as other magazines, Martin wrote that since the end of World War II, African-Americans who had fought for their country had come home to find that their rights as citizens were still being denied them. As a result, they had planted the seeds of unrest in their children's and grandchildren's minds and hearts. Now those same children and grandchildren were asking nothing more than their constitutional rights. "A generation of young people have come out of decades of shadows . . . [have] lost its fears . . . they are . . . replacing a dying order with a modern democracy," Martin wrote.

On an April weekend in 1960, Martin and Ella Baker who, because of her many talents and her capacity for hard work, had become the SCLC's acting director, met with two hundred students at Shaw University in North Carolina. At that gathering, Ms. Baker urged the students to form an organization that would tie together young people in every part of the country who were eager to work for justice and change. James Lawson, also called "the young people's Martin Luther King," and others, including Martin, also spoke. Before the weekend ended, the Student Nonviolent Coordinating Committee (SNCC) had been established. In the months that followed, Martin advised the new groups as they formed and did what he could to raise funds for their cause.

As news of the first sit-ins spread, students in cities throughout the South joined the effort. Throughout the summer and fall, they continued their nonviolent protests, despite injuries from angry bystanders and jailings by the police. Martin was cautious about participating in any student demonstrations in Atlanta, however, because he knew that older Negro leaders in the city, including his own father, disapproved of sit-ins and boycotts, fearing trouble from white people. A second reason for Martin's reluctance was that he had met twice with John F. Kennedy, the Massachusetts senator running for the presidency against Richard Nixon. Throughout his campaign, Kennedy had promised presidential support on civil rights issues, and he needed the black vote in order to win what he knew would be a close election. Martin felt that with only weeks to go before the election, any racial protest that caused trouble in Atlanta could echo around the country and cost Kennedy the presidency.

When SNCC students asked Martin to join mass sit-ins planned for late October in Atlanta, he declined. But the students persisted and Martin gave in. On a chilly Wednesday morning, he was arrested at a lunch counter in a downtown department store along with many others. The students were quickly released on a promise that the mayor would meet with store owners and city officials to discuss racial issues. But Martin was detained on another questionable charge and sentenced to four months at hard labor.

Late one night, he was awakened from a deep sleep by guards who handcuffed him, put him in leg chains, and rushed him off to Reidsville Penitentiary, three hundred miles from Atlanta. Thrown into a filthy, cockroach-infested cell, Martin knew that he was in deep trouble. Reidsville was a major center of Klan activity, and prison guards brutalized blacks, many of whom mysteriously disappeared. But after a few days, Martin was freed. Senator Kennedy had telephoned Coretta and promised to work for her husband's release. Robert Kennedy, the senator's brother and the future attorney general of the United States, had called the judge who had sentenced Martin, pleading for his release. John Kennedy won the November election in 1960, due in large part to the fact that three-fourths of the black voters in the country had voted for him.

In January 1961, Martin's third child, Dexter, was born. In the spring, a campaign to desegregate interstate buses and public facilities was begun by James Farmer and the Congress of Racial Equality. Fifteen years before, the Supreme Court had ordered buses and trains traveling across state lines to desegregate, but the ruling had been ignored in the South.

On a warm day in May, two buses carrying blacks and whites left Washington, D.C., bound for New Orleans, Louisiana. The passengers on the buses had spent three days in the capital, training for the nonviolent protest they were about to lead.

As the vehicles pulled out of the station, the people on board had no idea of what lay ahead on the thirteen-day journey southward. But they were full of hope, knowing that they were about to challenge one more barrier that denied them their freedom. James Farmer had named them the Freedom Riders.

In the beginning, there were no signs of trouble. Towns and cities passed by the windows. First, Fredericksburg and Richmond, Virginia. Then on into North and South Carolina. In Rock Hill, South Carolina, John Lewis, a future congressman from Georgia, and another man were beaten by thugs when they tried to enter a Whites Only restroom. Days later, as the buses pulled into a terminal just outside Anniston, Alabama, violence erupted when a screaming mob armed with bricks, clubs, and pipes slashed the tires of the first vehicle. Windows were smashed and a firebomb flew through a shattered window, starting a blaze that forced the Freedom Riders outside. As they came through the doors, the mob moved in on them, beating and bloodying them until they fell to the ground. A news reporter recording the event was heard to say, "These people are on fire for freedom!"

Later that month, another bus carrying Freedom Riders was attacked by a thousand whites in Montgomery. Again, people were brutally beaten.

On the evening of the violence, King, James Farmer, and other black leaders took to the pulpit of the church where Ralph Abernathy was now pastor to address a mass meeting protesting the beatings. As the leaders spoke, another mob rioted for hours outside the church, setting cars on fire and threatening to burn down the building. King made his way down to the basement where he phoned Attorney General Robert Kennedy. Within a short time federal marshals appeared, followed by state police and the National Guard.

Throughout the summer the Freedom Riders continued their peaceful protests. Many of the young people, members of the SNCC, were jailed repeatedly, causing others to object to Martin's absence on the rides. But Martin supported the students and their cause by working hard to raise money for their legal expenses and scholarships for those who would need help with college tuition the following autumn.

The Freedom Riders finally won their struggle in September 1961 when the Interstate Commerce Commission outlawed the segregation of public transportation facilities. But for many, the injuries they had endured would last a lifetime.

CHAPTER FIVE

"INJUSTICE ANYWHERE IS A THREAT TO JUSTICE EVERYWHERE"

By the spring of 1963, Martin Luther King Jr.'s accomplishments as the leader of the civil rights movement in the United States had won him international acclaim. Mail poured in from around the world, and requests for speaking engagements and interviews stretched his crowded schedule to the limit, leaving him little time to spend with his family and his writings. In spite of this, he managed to produce countless articles for major newsmagazines and traveled thousands of miles throughout the country to raise funds for SCLC and SNCC, and for

> **There were others who were putting their lives on the line to stand up for the constitutional rights that should have been the privilege of all Americans.**

scholarships benefitting worthy Negro college students. Since the publication of *Stride Toward Freedom* in 1958, *Strength to Love*, a collection of sermons presented before congregations in Montgomery and Atlanta, had appeared.

There were others, of course, who were putting their lives on the line in order to stand up for the constitutional rights that should have been the privilege of all Americans. As the movement continued, James Meredith became the first black student to enter the University of Mississippi. Harvey Gantt was enrolled at Clemson University in South Carolina, and Charlayne Hunter endured flying bricks and death threats to hold her place as a student at the University of Georgia.

From time to time there were setbacks, and not all demonstrations were successful. In Albany, Georgia, attempts to gain access to lunch counters failed and public transportation remained segregated. But Martin's work in Albany did much to raise the confidence of thousands of the city's black population who turned out for voter registration, resulting in the election of the first governor of Georgia to address civil rights issues.

New faces were emerging as the civil rights movement gained momentum in the nation. White students from around the country joined peaceful demonstrations and worked with the citizenship classes, teaching constitutional rights and encour-

Fannie Lou Hamer, shown here during one of her many speeches in support of civil rights for blacks, became one of the best-known leaders of the civil rights movement.

aging people to vote despite burdensome poll taxes and literacy tests.

One of the bravest of the new faces was a middle-aged black sharecropper from Mississippi named Fannie Lou Hamer. Arrested and beaten for trying to cast her ballot, Mrs. Hamer went on to become a tireless worker for the SNCC's voter registration program. Others, like Freedom Rider John Lewis (who later became the SNCC's chairman), Andrew Young, Jesse Jackson, Julian Bond, Charlayne Hunter, and Maya Angelou rose to national prominence in later years as political leaders, writers, journalists, and diplomats. Many people of all ages who became involved in the civil rights movement worked behind the scenes in those years. Their faces—and their names—have long since been forgotten.

The year 1963 marked the hundredth anniversary of President Abraham Lincoln's Emancipation Proclamation. Throughout the country, celebrations were held to honor the signing of the document that freed the slaves from bondage. But few of the people taking part in those celebrations understood the fact that while blacks had been freed from slavery, they were still not free to enjoy their constitutional rights. Nowhere in the country was this more evident than in the city of Birmingham, Alabama.

When the nation's schools were ordered to desegregate in 1954, one of Birmingham's political leaders defied the mandate by saying that "blood would run in the streets before desegregation would be permitted to come to Birmingham." Indeed, residents of the city welcomed the words of Alabama's new governor, George Wallace, in his inaugural address: "Segregation now! Segregation tomorrow! Segregation forever!"

In Birmingham, the schools, hospitals, churches, parks, neighborhoods, stores, and eating places—even elevators—were separated by the color of people's skin. The NAACP was banned from forming a local chapter, and the Metropolitan Opera had dropped the city from its tour schedule because its performers refused to appear before segregated audiences. There were no black policemen or firemen, and no jobs for blacks in white society other than as porters, laborers, gardeners, or maids.

Brutal acts of violence toward blacks went unpunished, and lynchings, drownings, bombings, kidnappings, and threats kept innocent people "in their place." In Birmingham, an atmosphere of fear existed in the heart of the black community, and no one perpetuated that fear more than Eugene "Bull" Connor, the city's commissioner of public safety.

But the African-American community was not without its leaders and prominent business and professional people. One of the most courageous of them was the Reverend Fred Shuttlesworth, the head of an organization called the Alabama Christian Movement for Human Rights. Shuttlesworth had been arrested eight times, his home and church had both been bombed, and when he and his wife tried to register their children in a white public school, a mob beat him with chains and brass knuckles and stabbed his wife. Because of his actions, the city council filed a $3 million lawsuit against Shuttlesworth and sold his home and car at a public auction.

For more than a year, Fred Shuttlesworth and his organization had boycotted a number of the city's stores and were now seeking the assistance of the SCLC. King and a group of his closest advisors, including Ralph Abernathy, met for three days in January to plan a strategy for confronting Bull Connor and his mobs. The third of April, 1963, was the target date set for the beginning of Project C, the code name for the confrontation. The plan included sit-ins, boycotts, rallies, mass marches, and mass meetings.

In the middle of all this, Martin's daughter, Bernice, was born on March 28. Then it all began. During the first of the sit-ins, Bull Connor's police hauled many of the participants off to jail and much of the black community, fearing retaliation from the whites, hesitated to join in the protest. But Martin was pleased to find swarms of reporters and television cameras ready to give national coverage to the campaign. If the demonstrators were to meet with violence, the country and the world would learn about it.

Project C included "freedom singers"—groups who gathered to march and sing freedom songs such as "We Shall Overcome."

*One of the many lunch counter sit-ins, conducted by
SNCC members in which young people would refuse to
leave an eating establishment until they were served*

At mass meetings held each night at several
of the city's black churches, Martin and his people
urged audiences to turn in weapons of violence
and taught everyone the protective tactics of nonviolent action. Each meeting produced growing

numbers of blacks willing to face Bull Connor's police; the determination of the people to act intensified. Within a week, hundreds of protesters had been arrested and quickly released with bond money supplied by Martin and the SCLC. The city of Birmingham in the meantime had issued an injunction against Martin and three other leaders, preventing them from demonstrating. In response, Martin declared that he would go to jail rather than call off the protest.

The next day, which was Good Friday—the most solemn day in the Christian calendar —Martin and Ralph Abernathy, along with Fred Shuttlesworth and other associates, marched through the center of Birmingham, stopping at the barricade where Bull Connor stood with his men. The police were everywhere: on rooftops, on foot, and in patrol cars. Martin and Abernathy knelt in prayer. A moment later, officers rushed up to both men, yanked at their shirts, and dragged them to a police wagon.

In jail by now for the thirteenth time, Martin found himself in solitary confinement in a cell worse than the one he had been placed in at Reidsville. Sitting on a narrow cot with no mattress, pillow, or blanket, he thought of all the brave people who had been jailed during the demonstrations and he worried about them. With so many taking part in the marches and sit-ins, there was no money left now to free them. "Those were the longest, most frustrating hours I have lived," Martin said. "I was in a nightmare of despair."

Several days later someone brought him a copy of the *Birmingham News*. In it was an article written and signed by eight of the city's clergymen, criticizing the Negro protests and praising Connor and the police for their patience in handling the demonstrators.

Writing along the margins of the newspaper and on scraps of paper brought by a prisoner trusty who brought his meals, Martin wrote his reply:

> I cannot sit idly by in Atlanta and not be concerned about what happens in Birmingham. Injustice anywhere is a threat to justice everywhere . . . whatever affects one directly, affects all indirectly . . . we have waited for more than 340 years for our constitutional and God-given rights . . . when you have seen vicious mobs lynch your mothers and fathers at will and drown your sisters and brothers at whim; when you have seen hate-filled policemen curse, kick and even kill your black brothers and sisters; when you see the vast majority of your twenty million Negro brothers smothering

in an airtight cage of poverty in the midst of an affluent society . . . when your first name becomes nigger, your middle name becomes boy . . . and your wife and mother are never given the respected title of Mrs. . . . then you will understand why we find it difficult to wait.

At the close of his letter, Martin wrote of the Negro's three hundred years of suffering:

Before the Pilgrims landed at Plymouth, we were here. Before the pen of Jefferson etched the majestic words of the Declaration of Independence . . . we were here . . . if the inexpressible cruelties of slavery could not stop us, the oppression we now face will surely fail. We will win our freedom because the sacred heritage of our nation and the eternal will of God are embodied in our echoing demands.

The letter was later smuggled out by King's lawyers one page at a time and submitted to the American Friends Service Committee, which quickly published "Letter from a Birmingham Jail." Within a short time, a million copies had been distributed, including those sent to the president, the attorney general, and other government officials.

One week later, NAACP lawyers posted bond money and Martin and Ralph Abernathy were released. But Martin discovered that without his leadership, the Birmingham protest had lost its enthusiasm. SNCC leaders in the meantime had been moving through the area's colleges and high schools to build support for the campaign. Why not bring them into the protest? Again, Martin was concerned: What if something happened to them?

The next day hundreds of high school students accompanied by hundreds of their younger sisters and brothers turned out for training sessions in nonviolent demonstration. Martin was hesitant about allowing the younger ones to participate but finally gave in to what later became known as the Children's Crusade.

Accompanied by adults and SNCC members, more than a thousand students, some of them as young as six years old, marched through the center of town clapping and singing the movement's most popular song, "We Shall Overcome." Watching the marchers as they approached the police barricades, an enraged Bull Connor ordered their arrest. As the youngsters climbed into the patrol wagons, a policeman turned to a little eight-year-old saying, "What do *you* want?" Without blinking an eye, the child answered, "Freedom!"

The following day, 2,500 children took to the streets. Martin urged them on, saying, "Don't get tired. Don't get bitter. Are you tired?"

"No," the children shouted back.

Marching with signs reading Freedom, the boys and girls headed for the barricades. As they came closer, Bull Connor ordered his firemen to turn on their hoses and the police to release their dogs.

What followed that hot, sultry April day made national and international headlines. Television cameras recorded the terrible sight of children and their leaders being slammed against sidewalks and buildings by the force of the water from the hoses. In homes throughout the country people watched in horror as police dogs ripped into the protesters' clothes. Many were severely bitten.

But the demonstrations continued and the numbers of children and their leaders swelled. With each march came the fire hoses and the dogs. And above the screaming and the noise came the voices of people singing freedom songs.

Between May 3 and May 10, with three thousand demonstrators crowding the city's jails and four thousand marching through the streets of Birmingham, negotiations between King's people and city officials began. On May 10, after days of heated discussion, an agreement was reached.

Black demonstrators attempt to shield themselves as firemen turn water hoses on them to break up their gathering. This photograph was taken in Birmingham, Alabama, on May 4, 1963.

Lunch counters and other public facilities would be desegregated within three months; within two months, blacks would be hired in jobs previously denied them; demonstrators would be released from the jails and a biracial committee would be formed to begin communications between black and white residents.

Violence erupted that night as Klansmen bombed A.D. King's home and threw a dynamite pack into the Gaston Motel where Martin had been staying. The trouble was not yet over, but the accords reached in Birmingham that spring marked a turning point in the history of the civil rights movement. The voices of the people had at last been heard.

CHAPTER SIX

"I HAVE A DREAM THAT ONE DAY ..."

The summer and fall of 1963 was a time of triumph and tragedy. On June 11, one month after the Birmingham agreement, a defiant Governor Wallace tried unsuccessfully to block the integration of the University of Alabama. That same night, President Kennedy addressed the nation to say that he was sending a civil rights bill to Congress, "on the principle that all men are created equal and that the rights of every man are diminished when the rights of one man are threatened." Minutes after the president concluded his speech, Medgar Evers, a civil rights leader in Jackson, Mississippi, was shot to death in the driveway of his home by a white racist.

Kennedy submitted his bill to Capitol Hill on June 19, deeply concerned about the continuing troubles in the South and the emergence of black hate groups such as those led by Elijah Muhammad's Nation of Islam. Three days later, Kennedy met in the Oval Office with civil rights leaders from the NAACP, CORE, the Urban League, and the SNCC. One of the topics discussed at the time was a plan for a march on Washington that was scheduled for late summer. The theme of the march would be a campaign for jobs and human rights.

The president was not happy about the idea. "We want success in Congress," Kennedy said, "not just a big show at the Capitol."

But civil rights leaders were determined to conduct the march, believing that a peaceful, non-violent show of strength supported by blacks and whites together would be a sign of unity, one that would bring people together and help to diminish the fires of racism. The date of the march was set for August 28, and the leading organizers of the event would be A. Philip Randolph and Bayard Rustin, the distinguished elders of the movement who had planned a similar march during the early 1940s when Franklin Delano Roosevelt had been president.

Meetings were held throughout July and August, and support for the march was building. More than one hundred religious, labor, and civil rights groups would be attending along with their representatives. Union leaders like Walter Reuther volunteered to act as sponsors, and more than 100,000 people were expected to arrive in Washington by way of buses, trains, and airplanes.

Preparations for an event of that size were clearly a challenge for the organizers. Planning the route of the march, providing water and food, restroom facilities, and medical assistance in the event of an emergency presented a multitude of concerns. At the top of everyone's mind was the belief that if the march were a success, it would demonstrate unity.

On the day of the march, a sea of people from all walks of life arrived in Washington. Tens of thousands came by buses and trains; members of a CORE chapter in New York actually had walked to the capital; and a biker from South Dakota and a roller skater from Chicago took their places in lines that were heading for the Lincoln Memorial. Blacks, whites, American Indians, Latinos, and Asian-Americans came to prove that this truly was a demonstration for human rights. Entertainers, musicians, and movie stars moved along with the crowds, eager to join in with the singing of the freedom songs. Television cameras rolled and a new communications satellite called Telstar sent a message of hope around the world as the proceedings got underway. As the day progressed the crowds grew to a half million people from all over

Martin Luther King Jr. addresses the crowd at the Lincoln Memorial during the August 28, 1963, March on Washington.

the country. On an enormous platform overlooking the audience, performers entertained and civil rights leaders spoke of a new day dawning. The last to speak was Martin Luther King Jr.

As thousands watched and listened in hushed silence, Martin's voice rose above the heads of the people. Toward the end of his address, the famous gospel singer Mahalia Jackson leaned toward him and said, "Tell them about the dream, Martin."

And Martin did:

I have a dream that one day on the red hills of Georgia sons of former slaves and the sons of former slave owners will be able to sit down together at the table of brotherhood. I have a dream that one day even the state of Mississippi, a state sweltering with the heat of injustice, sweltering with the heat of oppression, will be transformed into an oasis of freedom and justice. I have a dream that my four little children will live in a nation where they will not be judged by the color of their skin but by the content of their character. . . .

I have a dream today. . . .

This will be the day when all of God's children will be able to sing with new meaning "My country 'tis of thee, sweet land of liberty, of thee I sing" . . . let freedom ring from the . . . hilltops of New Hampshire. Let freedom ring from the mighty mountains of New York. Let freedom ring from the heightening Alleghenies of Pennsylvania . . . let freedom ring from Stone Mountain, Georgia. Let freedom ring from Lookout Mountain in Tennessee. Let freedom ring from every hill and molehill in Mississippi. "From every mountainside, let freedom ring."

When we allow freedom to ring . . . from every state and every city, we will be able to speed up that day when all of God's children, black men and white men, Jews and Gentiles, Protestants and Catholics, will be able to join hands and sing in the words of the old Negro spiritual, "Free at last! Free at last! Thank God almighty, we are free at last!"

Unity and harmony did prevail that memorable day in Washington, D.C. Not a shot was fired and no one was injured. The March on Washington sent a clear message to those who had doubted that a peaceful demonstration by 500,000 people could take place.

But three weeks later, tragedy struck again on Sunday, September 15. Four little girls—Addie May Collins, Denise McNair, Carole Robertson, and Cynthia Wesley—died when a bomb ripped through the Sixteenth Street Baptist Church in Birmingham. The theme of their Sunday School lesson that day was "The Love That Forgives." Twenty-one other children were injured in the blast.

Two months later in Dallas, Texas, President Kennedy was assassinated.

CHAPTER SEVEN

"NO LIE CAN LIVE FOREVER"

Deeply disturbed by the death of President Kennedy, Martin Luther King turned once again to his pen. In his third book, *Why We Can't Wait*, King wrote, "We were all involved in the death of John Kennedy. We tolerated hate; we tolerated the sick stimulation of violence in all walks of life." At the end of his book, he expressed his hope "that the sins of a dark yesterday will be redeemed in the achievements of tomorrow."

That kind of hope burned brightly in the minds of hundreds of volunteers from the South and the North who met in Mississippi to launch Freedom Schools, a civil rights program aimed at teaching blacks in that state lessons in civics, citizenship, reading, math, typing, and African-American history. The ultimate goal of the Freedom Schools was voter registration, a right that few Mississippi Negroes shared.

*A black woman in Mississippi concentrates on the
lesson in her Freedom School classroom.*

Learning of the schools, white racists across the state vowed vengeance on "Communists and outside agitators," and hate groups supported by local authorities. Phone threats and drive-by shootings occurred in the hundreds, and by the end of that summer, there had been more than a thousand arrests, eighty beatings, thirty bombings, and thirty-five church burnings and shootings. The most violent of the crimes occurred when three young men—Michael Schwerner, Andrew Goodman, and James Chaney—were murdered.

Tragic as that summer of 1964 was, one of the greatest successes of the civil rights movement came that same summer when President Lyndon B. Johnson signed the Civil Rights Act ending segregation in public schools, libraries, and playgrounds. The new law also banned discrimination in hiring practices and public accommodations.

In December of that year, millions of Americans and millions more abroad celebrated the awarding of the Nobel Peace Prize to Martin Luther King Jr. for his efforts to break down the walls of hatred by the nonviolent power of love.

While the 1964 Civil Rights Act granted blacks certain constitutional rights, it did not protect their right to vote. In cities and towns across the Deep South, poll taxes, literacy tests, violence, and the loss of jobs continued to keep blacks from registering and voting.

Early in 1965, an African-American organization in Selma, Alabama, contacted King to ask for his help in forming voter registration classes in their city. For close to a year, blacks in Selma had been trying to enter movie houses and other public accommodations now open to them with the passage of the Civil Rights Act and had been beaten and threatened by tear gas. Voter registration classes appeared out of the question.

By March the city was tense. A number of demonstrations by blacks and civil rights workers had been broken up by city and county officials using clubs and electric cattle prods, and a young

As the crowd pushed onward, they were attacked by an onrush of state police . . .

black army veteran had been fatally beaten. King himself had been attacked while trying to register at one of the city's hotels.

On Sunday, March 7, a group of about five hundred marchers gathered at the entrance of the Edmund Pettus Bridge leading out of town. Their goal was to mark the beginning of a mass march to Montgomery, the state capital, to take the injustices they were suffering straight to Governor Wallace's doorstep.

All was quiet but for the sounds of the people's footsteps. The leaders of the group, John Lewis and Hosea Williams, approached the middle of the humpbacked bridge. Suddenly, they stopped. The height of the Pettus Bridge had kept them from seeing the waves of helmeted state troopers carrying clubs and tear gas canisters. Several of them were wearing gas masks.

Lewis and Williams resumed their march and the people followed. When they reached the bottom of the bridge, the trooper in charge picked up a bullhorn and ordered them to turn back. As the crowd pushed onward, they were attacked by an onrush of state police pummeling them to the ground with billy clubs and fists. Then came the pop of tear gas canisters and the suffocating air that followed. Hundreds were injured that day as blood flowed onto the highway. Many, such as John Lewis, were hospitalized.

On the following day, members of both houses of Congress rose to protest Bloody Sunday. Several days later, President Johnson issued a statement to reporters:

The events of last Sunday cannot and will not be repeated . . . ninety-five years ago our Constitution was amended to require that no American be denied the right to vote because of race or color. . . . I will send to Congress a request for legislation.

The march to Montgomery took place with thousands of people participating. On that final day, speaking from an open square in front of the silver-and-white state capitol building, Martin Luther King Jr. spoke to the throng:

> I know some of you are asking today, "How long will it take?" . . . It will not be long, because truth pressed to the earth will rise again. . . . How long? Not long, because no lie can live forever. . . . Not long, because mine eyes have seen the coming of the Lord. . . . His truth is marching on.

The Voting Rights Act of 1965 was signed into law on August 6, one day shy of five months after Bloody Sunday. John Lewis later wrote that the passage of the law was "probably the nation's finest hour in terms of civil rights." A reporter suggested that the new law was a "brilliant climax which brought to a close the nonviolent struggle that reshaped the South."

CHAPTER EIGHT

"SAY THAT I WAS A DRUM MAJOR FOR JUSTICE"

During the final years of his life, Martin Luther King Jr. was deeply troubled by the racial violence that was sweeping the country. For three summers, riots had exploded in Los Angeles, New York, Detroit, Chicago, and countless other American cities. For some time, King had been warning that the "triple ghetto of race, poverty and human misery" would one day catch up with a nation that did little to solve its social problems.

Dr. King was equally disturbed by the emergence of Black Power leaders whose speeches were planting seeds of hatred encouraging the violence that was erupting in the cities. That kind of violence, he believed, was self-destructive.

There is nothing wrong with power if power is used correctly. . . . Nowhere have the riots won any [real] improvement such as have our organized protest demonstrations.

Martin Luther King Jr. and other members of a group called Clergy and Laymen Concerned About Vietnam conducted a vigil to protest the war in Vietnam on February 6, 1968.

In an address given in New York, Martin Luther King Jr. voiced his opposition to the war in Vietnam. "Today, young men of America are fighting, dying and killing in Asian jungles [and] are told they are sacrificing for democracy . . . and the black American soldier has himself never experienced democracy."

That kind of violence, he believed, was self-destructive.

Many people in the country—including some

of King's closest associates—were angered by his words, calling them un-American and irresponsible. Others, such as FBI director J. Edgar Hoover, believed him to be a Communist agitator. Because of this, Hoover's agents kept a close watch on King, wiretapping his telephones, planting electronic devices in his hotel rooms across the country, and keeping records of his every move.

Martin Luther King Jr.'s grueling schedule was taking a toll on him too. Continuing his crusade for justice and equality, he was now traveling more than 320,000 miles a year, giving as many as 450 major speeches annually, and coping with four hours or less of sleep each night. Despite this, King managed to write two more books, both of which were published in 1967. In *Where Do We Go from Here?* and *The Trumpet of Conscience,* he outlined the causes of the country's social ills and pointed to the need for peaceful change within what he called America's "beloved community."

One of King's greatest concerns in 1967 and the early months of 1968 was the problem of the undereducated and underpaid Negroes and white poor. Schools in the South and in the urban ghettos of the North lacked the educational programs that would give Negro and white students the education they needed in order to get decent jobs. In his campaign for jobs for the poor, King noted that the unemployment rate of young Negroes in many cities was as high as 40 percent. That figure was twice as high as that of the urban poor among whites.

By the fall of 1967, Martin Luther King was coming under increased criticism for his stand against the war in Vietnam. Many of the country's leading newspapers and newsmagazines were attacking him, as well as a number of veterans organizations. The Johnson administration denounced his opposition to the war as "right down the Commie line," and the FBI had stepped up its surveillance of his travels about the country.

Despite the criticism, King concentrated his efforts on the plight of America's underprivileged and called for a campaign that would "reach out to the poor people in all directions of the country," not only to African-Americans but to Latinos, American Indians, and Appalachians. Criticizing the Johnson administration for taking funds from its War on Poverty program to build up the war in Vietnam, he directed his aides to recruit three thousand citizens from ten of the nation's poorest urban and rural areas to work with the SCLC for three months of nonviolent action training. The Poor People's Campaign would later conduct a peaceful camp-in on the lawns of Lincoln Park across from the White House, urging friends and families to join with them to call attention to the need for jobs and income. While in Washington, people from the camp-in would meet with their congressional representatives to discuss the importance of immediate action. Many of King's associates thought that the demonstration would only draw increased anger from the Johnson administration, but King was determined to see it through and scheduled the camp-in for the following summer.

In the early months of 1968, as the war in Vietnam intensified and civil unrest continued to mount across the country, King's associates were increasingly worried about his welfare and his safety. Depressed by criticism from all directions and exhausted by the strain of his schedule, he talked frequently about the chance that he would not live much longer, telling his wife Coretta, "if anything happens to me, you must be prepared to continue." Coretta had already told a number of King's friends that she feared for her husband's life and had frequently dreamed that he would suffer a violent death. Preaching one of his last sermons at Ebenezer Baptist Church on February 4, King told his congregation:

Every now and then I think about my own death, and I think about my own funeral. . . . I ask myself, "What is it that I would want said." I'd like for somebody to say that day, that Martin Luther King Jr. tried to love somebody . . . that I tried to be right on the war question . . . that I did try to feed the hungry . . . that I tried to love and serve humanity . . . say that I was a drum major for justice . . . for peace . . . for righteousness.

Late in March, Martin Luther King Jr. answered a plea from striking sanitation workers in Memphis, Tennessee, to lead a peaceful protest through the streets of the city and to call attention to their demands for decent wages and benefits that had been denied them. The demonstration was planned for Friday, April 4.

Speaking in Memphis at a rally at Mason Temple, headquarters of the Church of God in Christ on the evening of April 3, King reminded his audience of the letter the young high school girl had written to him after he had been stabbed in New York, telling him that she was glad he had not sneezed:

If I had sneezed, I wouldn't have been here in 1963, when the black people of Birmingham, Alabama, aroused by the conscience of this nation, brought into being the Civil Rights Bill. If I had sneezed, I wouldn't have had a chance to tell Americans about a dream I had had. If I had sneezed, I wouldn't have been in Memphis to see a community rally around those brothers and sisters who are suffering.

To an audience of thousands who enthusiastically urged him on with responses such as, "Tell it, Doctor," and "Amen, Doctor," King told the people about a bomb threat on the plane that had brought him to Memphis that morning, and said:

Martin Luther King Jr. addressed the audience of striking sanitation workers on April 3, 1968, the night before his death.

Well, I don't know what will happen now. . . . But it doesn't matter to me now. Because I've been to the mountaintop. . . . Like anybody, I would like to live a long life . . . but I'm not concerned about that now. I just want to do God's will. And He's allowed me to go up to the mountain. And I've looked over. And I've seen the Promised Land. I may not get there with you. But I want you to know tonight that we, as a people, will get to the promised land. . . .

If any of you are around when I have to meet my day, I'd like somebody to mention . . . that Martin Luther King Jr. tried to give his life serving others. I'd like for somebody to say that day that Martin Luther King Jr. tried to love somebody. I want you to say that day that I tried to be right on the war question. I want you to be able to say that day, that I did try to feed the hungry. . . . I want you to say that I tried to love and serve humanity.

Yes, if you want to say that I was a drum major, say that I was a drum major for justice; say that I was a drum major for peace; I was a drum major for righteousness. . . . I just want to be there in love and in justice and in truth and in commitment to others, so that we can make of this old world a new world.

Early the next evening, April 4, 1968, as King and Andrew Young, along with Ralph Abernathy, Jessie Jackson, and other aides waited for a car to take them to a local minister's home for dinner, shots rang out through the air. Standing on the balcony of the Lorraine Motel in Memphis's black neighborhood, Martin Luther King Jr. was thrown to the concrete as an assassin's bullets struck him in the jaw and chest.

Rushed to the hospital in a desperate attempt to save his life, King died in the emergency room a short time later.

In his autobiography many years later, Andrew Young, a former congressman and ambassador to the United Nations, wrote of his work with King:

He left his mark on me, both in indelible memories and in the spiritual and practical lessons of our trials and triumphs. It is by the quality of those days that I have come to measure my own continuing journey.

Martin Luther King Jr. was not given the opportunity to realize his dream of one day returning to the academic world to teach. But in his work for the good of all people, he became—without realizing it—a great teacher and a man of vision and courage. He was indeed a drum major for justice.

This monument to Martin Luther King Jr., one of many forms of tribute to his memory that can be found throughout the country, stands on the campus of Morehouse College.

CHRONOLOGY

1929	Martin Luther King Jr. is born in Atlanta, Georgia, on January 15.
1944	Martin enters Morehouse College in Atlanta at the age of fifteen.
1946	President Truman appoints the President's Committee on Civil Rights. Moves to desegregate U.S. Armed Forces.
1947	Martin is ordained as a Baptist minister, becomes assistant pastor to his father at Ebenezer Baptist Church in Atlanta.
1948	Martin graduates from Morehouse College.
1951	Martin graduates from Crozer Theological Seminary.
1952	Martin meets Coretta Scott.
1953	Martin and Coretta are married on June 18.
1954	In April, Martin and Coretta Scott King

decide to accept pastorship of Dexter Avenue Baptist Church in Montgomery, Alabama. On May 17, the U.S. Supreme Court rules in *Brown* vs. *Board of Education* that public schools must be desegregated.

1955   Martin earns Ph.D. Supreme Court's "all deliberate speed" order on school integration announced. The Kings' first child, Yolanda, is born on November 17. Rosa Parks refuses to give up seat to white passenger on December 1. On December 5, the Montgomery Bus Boycott begins.

1956   Martin is convicted on boycott charges on March 22. In June, a federal court rules bus segregation unconstitutional. The ruling is upheld by the Supreme Court in November. On December 20, Montgomery, Alabama, mayor W.A. Gayle agrees to bus integration.

1957   Martin and others form the SCLC. On May 17, the Freedom Pilgrimage in Washington, D.C., takes place. On October 23, Martin Luther King III is born.

1958   *September 3:* Martin is arrested on false charge of disobeying a court officer. *September 5:* Martin is convicted and ordered to pay $10 fine or serve time in jail. When Martin chooses jail, the police commissioner pays the fine.

September 17: Stride Toward Freedom is published in New York.

September 20: Martin is stabbed by a mentally ill black woman in a Harlem bookstore.

1959   In February, Martin and Coretta tour Gandhian shrines in India, and Martin begins plans for further nonviolent demonstrations in the cause of civil rights. In November, Martin resigns as pastor of Dexter Avenue Baptist Church.

1960   *January:* Martin becomes associate pastor of Atlanta's Ebenezer Baptist Church.

February: Sit-ins by college students begin in Greensboro, North Carolina.

April: The Student Nonviolent Coordinating Committee (SNCC) is formed.

October: Martin is arrested for participating in Atlanta lunch counter sit-ins. He is sentenced to four months in jail on a false traffic violation; Robert Kennedy arranges for Martin's release.

1961   Dexter King is born in January. In May, the Freedom Rides begin.

1962   In October, James Meredith desegregates the University of Mississippi amidst rioting and injuries.

1963   *January:* George Wallace becomes Alabama governor; vows "segregation forever." King, Abernathy, and others meet with President Kennedy to learn he plans no civil rights action during 1963, despite urging by King and Abernathy.

March 28: Bernice King is born.

April 12: Martin is arrested for participation in Birmingham sit-ins; writes "Letter from a Birmingham Jail."

April 20: Martin is released from jail.

April/May: Martin joins Birmingham march; Bull Connor turns fire hoses and dogs on demonstrators; injuries and injustices covered by national television.

May 10: Birmingham agrees to desegregation.

June 11: Medgar Evers is killed in front of his Mississippi home.

August 28: March on Washington and "I Have a Dream" speech.

September 15: Four children die in Birmingham church bombing.

November 22: President Kennedy is assassinated in Dallas, Texas.

December: Strength to Love published.

1964   *July:* Civil Rights Act is signed into law; desegregation of public facilities and equal opportunity in hiring practices become law.

Summer: Civil rights workers James Chaney, Michael Schwerner, and Andrew Goodman are killed.

December: King receives the Nobel Peace Prize; President Johnson receives King at the White House, promises further civil rights action; *Why We Can't Wait* is published.

1965   *January:* King arrives in Selma, Alabama.

March: Bloody Sunday confrontation between marchers and police at Edmund Pettus Bridge. Two weeks later, King leads "March to Montgomery" protestors to Alabama state capitol.

August 6: Voting Rights Act is signed into law.

1967   Riots take place in Los Angeles, Detroit, Chicago, and other American cities. *Where Do We Go from Here?* and *The Trumpet of Conscience* are published. King begins plans for the Poor People's Campaign.

1968   *January:* King denounces war in Vietnam in speech at New York City's Riverside Church. Civil Rights Act barring discrimination in housing is passed.

February: King delivers his sermon at Ebenezer Baptist Church regarding his funeral.

April 3: King delivers his "Mountaintop" speech in Memphis.

April 4: King is assassinated at the Lorraine Motel in Memphis.

April 9: King's funeral takes place in Atlanta.

1983   President Ronald Reagan signs into law a bill to declare January 15, King's birthday, a federal holiday.

A NOTE ON SOURCES

A broad selection of sources assisted me in the writing of Dr. King's life and his involvement in the civil rights struggle. For example, there are more than a thousand Internet sites available to students, scholars, and researchers. In addition to the list in the For More Information section, there are many more books which time did not permit me to cover.

The huge collection of material on display at the King Center for Nonviolent Social Change in Atlanta, Georgia, is at this writing under negotiation for removal to one of the nation's leading universities. Another collection at Boston University houses more than 83,000 items about Dr. King up to about 1964. At Howard University in Washington, D.C., the Ralph J. Bunche Oral History Collection contains recorded interviews with Rosa

Parks, John Lewis, and many other civil rights leaders.

Several excellent films of Dr. King's life and his achievements can be found in video stores. A recent release is titled *Our Friend Martin—A Magical Adventure Inspired by the Life of MLK*. In January 1999, an excellent documentary on Martin Luther King Jr. decribing his leadership of the civil rights movement was aired on public television. Readers can order the film through local public television stations or video stores.

Also in January 1999, the King family, which had been in contact with Dr. King's convicted assassin, James Earl Ray, requested a formal reopening of the murder case, citing the discovery of new evidence and the statements of a number of law enforcement people still living who were involved in the case. Edward Pepper, a British barrister and a friend of Dr. King, wrote a controversial book on the subject, *Orders to Kill: The FBI and Martin Luther King, Jr.* Mr. Pepper eventually became Ray's final lawyer. The Associated Press International checked into Pepper's sources and "found that he represented them accurately." Because of the continuing controversy and the possibility of the case being reopened at some future date, however, I have not included Mr. Pepper's book in the bibliography.

FOR MORE INFORMATION

BOOKS

Colbert, Jan, and Ann McMillan Harms, eds. *Dear Dr. King: Letters from Today's Children to Dr. Martin Luther King, Jr.* Hyperion Books for Children, 1998.

Lusane, Clarence. *No Easy Victories: Black Americans and the Vote.* Franklin Watts, 1996.

Medearis, Angela Shelf. *Dare to Dream: Coretta Scott King and the Civil Rights Movement.* Lodestar, 1994.

Patterson, Lillie. *Martin Luther King, Jr. and the Freedom Movement.* Facts On File, 1989.

Rochelle, Belinda. *Witnesses to Freedom: Young People Who Fought for Civil Rights.* Lodestar, 1993.

ARTICLES

King, Rev. Bernice. "Keeping the Faith," *Ladies Home Journal,* January 1998.

King, Martin Luther, Jr. "Martin Luther King, Jr. Looks Ahead As New President of the Southern Christian Leadership Conference," *Jet,* January 19, 1998.

King, Yolanda. "Marching On," *People's Weekly,* January 18, 1999.

Shoulders, Lili. "Martin Luther King, Jr.," *Skipping Stones,* January–February 1998.

Smith, Vern E., and John Leland. "The Children Who Would Be King," *Newsweek,* April 6, 1998.

Smith, Vern E., and John Leland. "The War Over King's Legacy," *Newsweek,* April 6, 1998.

ORGANIZATIONS AND INTERNET RESOURCES

Dr. King's Home Church Finds a New Place to Nourish His Legacy

http: //web3.infotrac.galegroup.com

This site shows photographs of the new Ebenezer Baptist Church, built across the street from the original church. An article discusses a collection of Martin Luther King Jr. memorabilia housed in the new building.

Judgment Day for James Earl Ray

http: //www.conspire.com/curren28.html

This site is one of many sources that look into the question of whether or not there was a conspiracy to kill Dr. King.

Martin Luther King Jr.
http://www.familyeducation.com
This site provides a wide selection of resources on Martin Luther King Jr. that can be enjoyed by the entire family. In addition to photographs, there are articles and projects for all ages.

The Martin Luther King Jr. Center for Nonviolent Social Change.
449 Auburn Avenue NE
Atlanta, GA 30312
http://www.thekingcenter.com
This site gives information on the collections of King's written works, speeches, and much more, including the center's telephone and fax numbers as well as days of the week the center is open for touring or for study.

Martin Luther King Jr., 1929–1968
http://www.angelfire.com
This site can provide another glimpse into the world of Martin Luther King Jr. and his achievements.

INDEX

▲ 109 ▲

ABOUT THE AUTHOR

Jayne Pettit is the author of several children's books, including *Michelangelo: Genius of the Renaissance* and *Jane Goodall: Pioneer Researcher.* She holds a master's degree in education and has taught in the public and independent schools for twenty years. In addition to her writing career, she works with Latino adults, teaching English as a second language. She has three grown children, seven grandchildren, and lives with her husband on Hilton Head Island, South Carolina.

Due Back
Feb. 4, '04